# Unveiling Encrypted World

# Your Comprehensive Guide to Launching a Cybersecurity Career

Benjamin Evans

# DEDICATION

To the relentless seekers of knowledge, the curious minds tirelessly decoding the mysteries of algorithms and code. This book is dedicated to you, the coders who embrace the challenges of neural networks with fervor and determination. May these pages serve as stepping stones on your journey, empowering you to unravel the complexities of this dynamic field and craft solutions that shape the future. Your passion fuels the innovation that drives our world forward, and for that, I extend my deepest gratitude and admiration.

# CONTENTS

# ACKNOWLEDGMENTS

I would like to extend my sincere gratitude to all those who have contributed to the realization of this book. First and foremost, I am indebted to my family for their unwavering support and encouragement throughout this endeavor. Their love and understanding have been my anchor in the stormy seas of writing.

I am deeply thankful to the experts whose guidance and insights have illuminated my path and enriched the content of this book. Their mentorship has been invaluable in shaping my understanding and refining my ideas.

I also extend my appreciation to those whose constructive feedback and insightful suggestions have helped polish this work to its finest form.

Furthermore, I am grateful to the countless individuals whose research, publications, and contributions have paved the way for the insights shared in these pages.

Last but not least, I express my heartfelt appreciation to the readers who embark on this journey with me. Your curiosity and engagement breathe life into these words, and it is for you that this book exists.

Thank you all for being part of this remarkable journey.

# CHAPTER 1

Welcome to the exciting world of cybersecurity! In this chapter, we'll delve into the fundamentals of this critical field, exploring what it is, why it matters, and the vast career opportunities it offers.

## 1.1 What is Cybersecurity?

Cybersecurity, in its simplest form, is the practice of protecting networks, systems, and data from unauthorized access, use, disclosure, disruption, modification, or destruction. Imagine a fortress safeguarding your valuable information. Cybersecurity encompasses the tools, policies, processes, and people dedicated to building and maintaining those digital defenses.

**Breaking it Down:**

- **Networks:** The interconnected systems that allow us to communicate and share information. This includes computers, servers, routers, and other devices.

- **Systems:** Software applications, databases, and operating systems essential for businesses and individuals.

- **Data:** The digital information we create, store, and transmit, including personal details, financial records, intellectual property, and more.

**The Three Pillars of Cybersecurity:**

The CIA Triad (Confidentiality, Integrity, and Availability) serves as a foundational principle in cybersecurity.

- **Confidentiality:** Ensuring only authorized users can access sensitive data. Imagine a locked safe for your most critical information.

- **Integrity:** Protecting data from unauthorized modification or alteration. Think of a secure system that ensures information remains accurate and consistent.

- **Availability:** Guaranteeing authorized users have timely and reliable access to systems and data. This means critical information is accessible whenever needed.

## 1.2 The Evolving Threat Landscape

Unfortunately, the digital world isn't always safe. Cybercriminals are constantly developing new methods to exploit vulnerabilities in our systems and gain access to valuable information. The threat landscape is constantly evolving, with new attack vectors emerging regularly.

**Common Threats:**

- **Malware:** Malicious software like viruses, worms, and ransomware designed to disrupt, steal, or damage data.
- **Phishing Attacks:** Deceptive emails or websites that trick users into revealing sensitive information.

- **Social Engineering:** Exploiting human psychology to manipulate users into giving up access credentials or confidential data.

- **Hacking:** Unauthorized attempts to gain access to a system or network for malicious purposes.

These threats can have devastating consequences, causing financial losses, reputational damage, data breaches, and disruption to critical services.

**Why Threats Keep Evolving:**

Cybercriminals are motivated by a variety of factors, including financial gain, espionage, and even activism. As technology advances and our reliance on digital systems increases, the potential rewards for attackers become greater, driving them to develop more sophisticated methods.

## 1.3 Why is Cybersecurity Important?

Cybersecurity is no longer a niche concern; it's a

fundamental aspect of our digital lives. Here's why it matters:

- **Protecting Personal Information:** Our personal data, including financial records, medical history, and online identities, are vulnerable to cyberattacks. Robust cybersecurity helps safeguard this sensitive information.

- **Ensuring Business Continuity:** Businesses rely heavily on their digital infrastructure. Cyberattacks can disrupt operations, cause financial losses, and damage customer trust. Effective cybersecurity is critical for business continuity.

- **Safeguarding Critical Infrastructure:** Cyberattacks can target vital infrastructure like power grids, transportation systems, and financial institutions, posing a threat to national security and public safety. Robust cybersecurity helps protect these systems.

- **Maintaining Trust and Privacy:** Data breaches and

privacy violations can erode trust in online services and institutions. Strong cybersecurity practices demonstrate a commitment to protecting user data and privacy.

The increasing dependence on digital technologies makes cybersecurity more crucial than ever before. By securing our systems and data, we can build a more secure and resilient digital future.

## 1.4 Career Opportunities in Cybersecurity

Cybersecurity is a rapidly growing field offering a vast array of exciting career paths. Here's just a glimpse of the opportunities available:

- **Security Analyst:** Monitors networks and systems for suspicious activity, investigates security incidents, and responds to threats.

- **Penetration Tester:** Ethical hackers who identify vulnerabilities in systems by simulating real-world attacks.

- **Security Architect:** Designs and implements secure network architectures and security protocols.

- **Security Engineer:** Develops and maintains security tools and technologies to protect systems and data.

- **Cybersecurity Consultant:** Advises organizations on developing and implementing effective cybersecurity strategies.

- **Digital Forensics Investigator:** Analyzes digital evidence to investigate cybercrimes and identify perpetrators.

These are just a few examples. The diverse field of cybersecurity offers a variety of career options for individuals with different skills and interests. It's a field that provides intellectual challenges, opportunities for continuous learning, and the satisfaction of contributing to a safer digital world.

# CHAPTER 2

## BUILDING A FOUNDATION

Now that you're excited about the world of cybersecurity, it's time to lay the groundwork for your journey. This chapter focuses on building a solid foundation of knowledge and skills that will equip you for success.

## 2.1 Understanding Your Learning Style

Everyone learns differently. Recognizing your preferred learning style allows you to choose educational resources and methods that best suit your needs. Here are some common learning styles:

- **Visual Learners:** Absorb information best through images, diagrams, and videos. Online courses with infographics, animations, and video demonstrations cater well to this style.

- **Auditory Learners:** Benefit most from lectures, podcasts, and audiobooks. Look for resources that offer audio explanations and discussions.

- **Kinesthetic Learners:** Learn best by doing. Hands-on labs, simulations, and practical exercises are ideal for this style. Consider setting up a home lab environment to practice your skills.

- **Reading/Writing Learners:** Prefer written text and enjoy taking notes. Textbooks, articles, and online tutorials cater well to this style.

**Tips for Identifying Your Learning Style:**

- Reflect on past learning experiences. What methods helped you grasp information most effectively?

- Take online quizzes or assessments designed to identify learning styles.

- Experiment with different resources and see which resonate with you.

**Embrace a Blended Approach:**

Most people are a combination of different learning styles. Don't limit yourself to just one method. Utilize a blend of resources to maximize your learning potential.

## 2.2 Essential Technical Skills

Cybersecurity professionals rely on a strong technical foundation. Here are some key skills to focus on:

### 2.2.1 Networking Fundamentals

Understanding how networks function is crucial for cybersecurity. You'll need to grasp concepts like:

- **Network Topologies (Bus, Star, Mesh, etc.):** Different network configurations and their strengths and weaknesses.
- **Network Devices (Routers, Switches, Firewalls):** The functionality of these devices and their role in network security.

- **IP Addressing (IPv4, IPv6):** The system for uniquely identifying devices on a network.

- **TCP/IP Protocol Suite:** This communication protocol that governs how data travels across networks.

## Learning Resources:

- Free online courses like "Introduction to Networks" on platforms like Coursera and edX.

- Textbooks like "Computer Networking: A Top-Down Approach" by James Kurose and Keith Ross.

### 2.2.2 Operating Systems

Operating systems are the software platforms that manage computer hardware resources. Familiarize yourself with popular operating systems like:

- **Windows:** Widely used desktop and server operating system.

- **Linux:** A powerful and versatile open-source operating system. Understanding Linux commands is valuable in cybersecurity.

- **MacOS:** The operating system used on Apple computers.

**Learning Resources:**

- Online tutorials and guides for specific operating systems.

- Consider installing a virtual machine to experiment with different operating systems in a safe environment.

- Free online resources like "TryHackMe" offer virtual labs to practice Linux commands.

## 2.2.3 Programming Languages (e.g., Python, Bash)

Having basic programming knowledge is a valuable asset in cybersecurity. Here's why:

- **Automation:** Writing scripts can automate repetitive

tasks, saving time and reducing human error.

- **Security Tools:** Many cybersecurity tools utilize scripting languages. Knowing Python or Bash allows you to customize and extend their functionality.

- **Understanding Malicious Code:** Basic programming knowledge helps you analyze suspicious code and understand its potential impact.

**Learning Resources:**

- Online coding platforms like Codecademy offer beginner-friendly courses in Python and Bash scripting.

- Free online tutorials and interactive coding challenges.

- Consider enrolling in a programming bootcamp for a more intensive learning experience.

These are just the foundational skills. As you delve deeper into cybersecurity, you'll explore more specialized areas like cryptography, security protocols, and vulnerability assessment. The key is to start building a solid foundation of knowledge and practice, which will serve you well as you progress on your cybersecurity journey.

## 2.3 Developing Critical Thinking and Problem-Solving Skills

The world of cybersecurity is a constant battle against evolving threats. Success requires more than just technical expertise. You'll need to be a critical thinker and problem solver to effectively analyze situations, identify vulnerabilities, and develop solutions.

Here's how to hone these crucial skills:

- **Question Everything:** Don't take things at face value. Develop a healthy skepticism and critically analyze information presented to you.
- **Break Down Problems:** When faced with a security incident, learn to break it down into smaller, more manageable components. Identify the root cause and potential consequences.

- **Consider Different Perspectives:** Analyze a problem from multiple angles. Consider how attackers might exploit vulnerabilities and the potential impact on different stakeholders.

- **Think Outside the Box:** Don't settle for the first solution that comes to mind. Explore unconventional approaches and creative solutions.

- **Practice Makes Perfect:** Engage in activities that promote critical thinking, such as logic puzzles, ethical hacking challenges (Capture the Flag – CTFs), and security case studies.

**Benefits of Strong Critical Thinking and Problem-Solving Skills:**

- **Effective Incident Response:** These skills equip you to react quickly and efficiently to security threats.

- **Proactive Security Measures:** You can anticipate potential issues and develop preventive measures to mitigate risks.

- **Staying Ahead of Attackers:** Thinkers who can anticipate attacker strategies are more likely to design robust defenses.

- **Adaptability in a Changing Landscape:** As threats evolve, your critical thinking allows you to adapt and adjust your approach.

## 2.4 Cultivating a Security Mindset

Cybersecurity isn't just about technical tools; it's also about adopting a specific way of thinking. Cultivating a security mindset means constantly being aware of potential threats and taking steps to mitigate them.

Here are some ways to develop this mindset:

- **Security is Everyone's Responsibility:** Cybersecurity isn't just for IT professionals. Everyone within an organization needs to be aware of security best practices.

- **Think Like an Attacker:** Try to see things from the

perspective of a cybercriminal. This will help you identify your vulnerabilities and understand where attackers might focus their efforts.

- **Be Proactive, Not Reactive:** Don't wait for a security incident to happen before taking action. Develop a proactive approach that emphasizes prevention and preparedness.

- **Develop a Healthy Dose of Paranoia:** While not everything is a threat, be cautious when dealing with online information and unknown sources.

- **Stay Informed:** Keep yourself updated on the latest cybersecurity threats, vulnerabilities, and best practices.

**Benefits of a Security Mindset:**

- **Reduced Security Risks:** By being constantly vigilant, you can identify and address potential issues before they escalate into major problems.

- **Improved Decision-Making:** A security mindset allows you to make informed decisions that consider potential security implications.

- **Building a Culture of Security:** When everyone within an organization prioritizes security, it becomes embedded in the overall culture.

By developing critical thinking, problem-solving skills, and a security mindset, you'll be well-equipped to navigate the ever-changing cybersecurity landscape and contribute to a more secure digital future.

# CHAPTER 3

## Core Cybersecurity Concepts

You've established a strong foundation in learning styles and essential technical skills, it's time to delve into the core concepts of cybersecurity. Understanding these fundamental principles will equip you to recognize threats and implement effective security measures.

## 3.1 The CIA Triad: Confidentiality, Integrity, Availability

The CIA Triad is a foundational principle in cybersecurity that serves as a framework for understanding security objectives. It emphasizes the importance of protecting three critical aspects of information:

- **Confidentiality:** This principle ensures that only authorized users can access sensitive data. Imagine a locked safe or secure online storage system that restricts access to your personal information.

- **Integrity:** This principle safeguards data from unauthorized modification or alteration. Think of checksums or digital signatures that verify data hasn't been tampered with during transmission or storage.

- **Availability:** This principle guarantees that authorized users have timely and reliable access to information and systems. Think of a functioning website that users can access readily whenever needed.

Cybersecurity professionals strive to maintain a balance between these three objectives. Implementing robust security measures might impact one aspect slightly, but the overall goal is to achieve an optimal balance that protects information effectively.

## 3.2 Threat Actors and Their Motivations

Unfortunately, the digital world isn't all sunshine and rainbows. Malicious actors constantly seek to exploit vulnerabilities in our systems and data for various reasons. Let's explore some of the most common threat actors and their motivations:

- **Cybercriminals:** These individuals or groups aim to steal financial information, intellectual property, or personal data for financial gain. They might sell stolen data on the black market or use it for identity theft or fraud.

- **Hacktivists:** These are individuals or groups who use cyberattacks to promote a political or social agenda. They might deface websites, disrupt critical infrastructure, or leak sensitive information to raise awareness for their cause.

- **State-Sponsored Actors:** Certain governments sponsor cyberattacks to gain intelligence, disrupt critical infrastructure of other nations, or influence political outcomes.

- **Disgruntled Insiders:** Employees or former employees with access to a system might launch attacks out of revenge, protest, or for personal gain.

Understanding the motivations behind cyberattacks helps us anticipate potential threats and implement targeted security measures.

## 3.3 Common Attack Vectors and Techniques

Threat actors utilize various means to gain unauthorized access to systems and data. Understanding these common attack vectors and techniques is crucial for effective defense. Here are a few examples:

### 3.3.1 Social Engineering:

This tactic exploits human psychology to manipulate users into revealing sensitive information or taking actions that compromise security. Here's how it works:

- **Phishing Attacks:** Deceptive emails or messages

designed to trick users into clicking malicious links or attachments that download malware or redirect them to fake login pages.

- **Pretexting:** Impersonating a trusted entity (e.g., bank, IT support) to trick users into disclosing personal information or granting access to systems.
- **Tailgating:** Gaining unauthorized physical access to a secure location by following a legitimate user.

Social engineering attacks are often successful because they prey on human trust and inattentiveness. It's important to be aware of these tactics and develop a healthy dose of skepticism towards unsolicited messages and requests.

### 3.3.2 Malware:

Malicious software designed to disrupt, steal, or damage data. Malware can take various forms, including:

- **Viruses:** Self-replicating programs that spread from one computer to another, infecting systems and potentially causing damage.

- **Worms:** Similar to viruses, but propagate without needing a host program.

- **Trojan Horses:** Disguised programs that appear legitimate but perform malicious actions upon execution.

- **Ransomware:** This type of malware encrypts a user's data and demands a ransom payment to decrypt it.

Malware can be distributed through various means like infected email attachments, malicious websites, or physical devices like USB drives. Implementing anti-malware software and practicing safe browsing habits are essential to mitigate these threats.

### 3.3.3 Phishing Attacks:

We mentioned phishing attacks briefly under social engineering. These deceptive emails or messages attempt to trick users into revealing sensitive information or clicking malicious links. Phishing emails often:

- **Appear to be from legitimate sources:** They might mimic emails from banks, credit card companies, or social media platforms.

- **Create a sense of urgency:** They might pressure users to act quickly by claiming an account is compromised or a payment is overdue.

- **Contain typos or grammatical errors:** Be wary of emails with unprofessional language, as legitimate companies typically maintain high standards for communication.

- Don't click on suspicious links or attachments in emails. Hover over links to see the actual destination URL before clicking.

- Be cautious of unsolicited emails, even if they appear to be from a known company.

- Verify the sender's email address carefully. Legitimate companies won't use generic email addresses like "[email address removed]" to request sensitive information.

- Never enter personal information or login credentials

on websites accessed through links in emails. Legitimate institutions will direct you to their secure login pages directly.

- If unsure about an email's legitimacy, contact the sender directly through a trusted phone number or website (not the one provided in the email).

By understanding social engineering tactics and being vigilant about phishing attempts, you can significantly reduce the risk of falling victim to these attacks.

## 3.4 Introduction to Security Controls and Best Practices

Now that you're familiar with common threats and attack vectors, it's time to explore how we defend ourselves. Security controls and best practices are the measures implemented to safeguard systems and data. Here are some fundamental examples:

- **Access Control:** This ensures only authorized users have access to specific systems and data based on their roles and permissions. Examples include password protection, multi-factor authentication (MFA), and access control lists (ACLs).

- **Network Security:** Firewalls, intrusion detection/prevention systems (IDS/IPS), and network segmentation are implemented to monitor and control network traffic, identify suspicious activity, and prevent unauthorized access.

- **Data Security:** Encryption safeguards sensitive data at rest and in transit, rendering it unreadable by unauthorized individuals. Data backups are also crucial for disaster recovery in case of attacks or system failures.

- **Vulnerability Management:** Regularly scanning systems for vulnerabilities and patching them promptly is essential to address potential weaknesses before attackers exploit them.

- **Security Awareness Training:** Educating users about cyber threats, social engineering tactics, and best practices is vital. A well-informed workforce can significantly enhance an organization's overall security posture.

These are just a few examples, and the specific security controls implemented will vary depending on the organization's size, industry, and risk profile. However, by adopting a layered approach that combines technical controls, best practices, and user awareness training, organizations can significantly strengthen their defenses against cyberattacks.

# CHAPTER 4

It's time to explore how you can validate your knowledge and enhance your career prospects. This chapter dives into the world of entry-level cybersecurity certifications.

## 4.1 CompTIA Security+

CompTIA Security+ is a vendor-neutral certification that serves as a foundational credential for aspiring cybersecurity professionals. It validates your core knowledge and skills in network security, systems security, cryptography, and security risks.

**Exam Overview and Content Areas:**

CompTIA Security+ covers a broad range of topics, including:

- **Network Security:** Firewalls, intrusion detection/prevention systems, network segmentation, and secure communication protocols.

- **Cloud Security:** Security considerations for cloud-based environments and data storage.

- **Identity and Access Management (IAM):** User authentication, authorization, and access control mechanisms.

- **Risk Management:** Identifying, assessing, and mitigating security risks.

- **Incident Response:** Procedures for handling security breaches and cyberattacks.

- **Security Architecture and Design:** Secure system design principles and best practices.

- **Cryptography:** Encryption techniques and their role in protecting data confidentiality.

These are just some of the core areas covered in the exam. Passing the CompTIA Security+ demonstrates your understanding of essential cybersecurity concepts and positions you for entry-level security analyst roles.

**Preparation Tips and Resources:**

- **Official CompTIA Security+ Website:** This website provides information about the exam, including the exam objectives, study resources, and recommended training materials.

- **CompTIA Security+ Study Guides and Practice Tests:** Numerous books, online courses, and practice tests are available from reputable publishers and training providers.

- **Bootcamps:** Intensive bootcamps can deliver a comprehensive review of the exam objectives in a short period.

- **Online Communities and Forums:** Participating in online communities and forums allows you to connect with other Security+ candidates, ask questions, and share study tips.

**Tips for Success:**

- **Develop a Study Plan:** Create a comprehensive study plan that allocates time for each exam domain.

- **Practice, Practice, Practice:** Take advantage of practice tests to identify knowledge gaps and track your progress.

- **Join a Study Group:** Studying with others can keep you motivated and provide a platform for knowledge exchange.

- **Stay Focused and Motivated:** Earning a certification requires dedication and hard work. Maintain focus on your goals and celebrate your achievements.

## 4.2 Other Entry-Level Certifications

While CompTIA Security+ is a popular starting point, various other entry-level certifications cater to specific areas within cybersecurity. Here are two examples:

### 4.2.1 (ISC)² Certified Secure Incident Analyst (CSA+):

This certification focuses on developing skills in incident response, threat detection, and security operations. It's ideal for individuals interested in pursuing careers as security analysts, incident responders, or security operations center (SOC) analysts.

## 4.2.2 GIAC Security Essentials (GSEC):

This certification provides a broad foundational knowledge of information security and risk management. It's a vendor-neutral credential that can be a stepping stone towards more advanced GIAC certifications in specific security domains.

These are just a few examples, and the best choice for you will depend on your career aspirations and interests. Researching various entry-level certifications and their corresponding job roles will help you select the one that best aligns with your career goals.

## 4.3 Choosing the Right Certification for You

The cybersecurity field offers a diverse range of career paths. Choosing the right entry-level certification depends on several factors:

- **Career Goals:** What specific area of cybersecurity interests you most? (e.g., network security, incident response, security architecture)

- **Learning Style:** Do you prefer a vendor-neutral certification with broad coverage or one focused on specific tools and platforms?

- **Exam Difficulty:** Consider your current knowledge base and the time commitment required to prepare for different exams.

- **Industry Demand:** Certain industry verticals might favor specific certifications depending on their security needs.

**Here's a tip:**

- Many resources online offer comparison charts outlining the key features of different entry-level certifications. Utilize these resources to compare and contrast options based on your individual needs.

## 4.4 Value of Entry-Level Certifications

Earning an entry-level cybersecurity certification offers several benefits:

- **Validates Your Knowledge:** Certifications demonstrate your understanding of fundamental security concepts and best practices.
- **Enhances Your Resume:** Certifications stand out to potential employers, showcasing your commitment to professional development.
- **Boosts Your Credibility:** Certifications lend credibility to your skills and knowledge in the job market.
- **Provides Career Flexibility:** Certifications can open doors to various entry-level security analyst positions.
- **Serves as a Stepping Stone:** Many advanced

cybersecurity certifications require holding a foundational credential like Security+. Earning an entry-level certification positions you for further career advancement within the field.

- **Increases Earning Potential:** Studies suggest that cybersecurity professionals with certifications can command higher salaries compared to their non-certified counterparts.

**Remember:** Certifications alone won't guarantee a job. However, they demonstrate your dedication to the field and provide a valuable foundation for a successful cybersecurity career.

The world of cybersecurity certifications can seem overwhelming at first. However, by understanding the various options, assessing your career goals, and utilizing the available resources, you can select the right entry-level certification to kickstart your journey. As you gain experience and knowledge, you can explore more advanced certifications to further specialize and excel in your chosen cybersecurity domain.

This chapter has equipped you with a roadmap to navigate the landscape of entry-level cybersecurity certifications.

# CHAPTER 5

## EXPLORING DIFFERENT CYBERSECURITY PATHS

It's time to delve into the diverse career paths this exciting field offers. This chapter will introduce you to some of the most popular specializations within cybersecurity.

## 5.1 Network Security

Network security professionals are the gatekeepers of an organization's digital infrastructure. They are responsible for securing computer networks, protecting them from unauthorized access, and mitigating cyber threats.

## 5.1.1 Firewalls and Intrusion Detection/Prevention Systems (IDS/IPS):

- **Firewalls:** These act as the first line of defense,

49

filtering incoming and outgoing network traffic based on predefined security rules. Network security professionals configure, maintain, and monitor firewalls to ensure smooth operation and effective threat detection.

- **Intrusion Detection/Prevention Systems (IDS/IPS):** These systems continuously monitor network activity for suspicious behavior that might indicate a cyberattack. IDS systems alert security analysts to potential threats, while IPS systems can actively block malicious traffic. Network security professionals configure, maintain, and analyze alerts generated by these systems.

### 5.1.2 Network Security Monitoring and Analysis:

Network security professionals utilize various tools and techniques to monitor network traffic for anomalies and suspicious activity. This includes:

- **Traffic analysis:** Identifying unusual patterns in

network traffic that might indicate a cyberattack.

- **Log analysis:** Examining logs generated by network devices and security tools to identify potential security incidents.

- **Vulnerability scanning:** Regularly scanning systems for known vulnerabilities that attackers might exploit.

By analyzing network activity and identifying potential threats, network security professionals play a vital role in protecting an organization's critical infrastructure.

## 5.2 Security Operations Center (SOC) Analyst

Security Operations Centers (SOCs) are the nerve centers of an organization's security posture. SOC analysts work around the clock to monitor security systems, detect threats, and respond to security incidents.

### 5.2.1 Incident Response and Threat Hunting:

- **Incident Response:** When a security breach occurs,

SOC analysts follow established procedures to contain the damage, eradicate the threat, and recover compromised systems. They analyze incident data, identify the root cause, and implement mitigation strategies.

- **Threat Hunting:** Beyond waiting for threats to emerge, SOC analysts proactively search for hidden threats within the network. This proactive approach utilizes various tools and techniques to identify potential threats before they can cause disruption or damage.

## 5.2.2 Security Information and Event Management (SIEM):

SOC analysts rely heavily on Security Information and Event Management (SIEM) tools. SIEM aggregates security data from various sources, including firewalls, intrusion detection systems, and endpoint security tools.

This consolidated view allows analysts to identify patterns, correlate events, and detect potential threats more effectively.

The role of a SOC analyst requires a blend of technical skills, analytical thinking, and the ability to work effectively under pressure in a fast-paced environment.

## 5.3 Penetration Testing and Ethical Hacking

Penetration testers, also known as ethical hackers, are authorized individuals who employ the same techniques as malicious hackers to identify vulnerabilities in an organization's systems and networks.

## 5.3.1 Vulnerability Assessment and Penetration Testing (VAPT):

- **Vulnerability Assessment:** This involves identifying weaknesses and potential security flaws in systems and applications using automated tools and manual techniques.

- **Penetration Testing:** Ethical hackers attempt to exploit identified vulnerabilities to gain unauthorized access to systems and data, simulating real-world cyberattacks. This helps organizations understand the potential impact of vulnerabilities and prioritize remediation efforts.

### 5.3.2 Tools and Techniques for Ethical Hackers:

Ethical hackers utilize a vast arsenal of tools and techniques, including:

- **Security scanners:** Automated tools that identify vulnerabilities in systems and applications.
- **Social engineering techniques:** Simulating phishing attacks or other social engineering tactics to test an organization's awareness and preparedness.
- **Exploit kits:** Software tools that take advantage of known vulnerabilities to gain unauthorized access.

By mimicking the methods of malicious actors, ethical hackers play a crucial role in strengthening an organization's security posture by identifying and addressing vulnerabilities before they can be exploited by real attackers.

## 5.4 Other Cybersecurity Specializations

The exciting world of cybersecurity offers a variety of career paths beyond the ones explored in this chapter. Here are a few additional specializations to consider:

- **Security Analyst:** This is a broad role encompassing various security tasks, including vulnerability management, incident response, and user security awareness training.

- **Security Architect:** These individuals design and implement secure network architectures, ensuring systems and data are protected from unauthorized access.

- **Digital Forensics Investigator:** They specialize in collecting, analyzing, and preserving digital evidence in the case of cybercrimes.

- **Cloud Security Specialist:** As cloud adoption grows, professionals with expertise

- **Cloud Security Specialist:** As cloud adoption grows, professionals with expertise in securing cloud environments are increasingly in demand. This specialization requires an understanding of cloud computing platforms like AWS, Azure, and GCP, along with knowledge of cloud security best practices.

- **Security Analyst:** This is a broad role encompassing various security tasks, including vulnerability management, incident response, and user security awareness training. Security analysts often work within SOCs and play a vital role in maintaining an organization's overall security posture.

- **Security Architect:** These individuals design and implement secure network architectures, ensuring systems and data are protected from unauthorized access. Security architects possess a deep understanding of security principles, network technologies, and risk management strategies.

- **Digital Forensics Investigator:** They specialize in collecting, analyzing, and preserving digital evidence in the case of cybercrimes. Digital forensics investigators play a crucial role in cybercrime investigations by recovering and analyzing electronic data from compromised systems.

- **Cyber Threat Intelligence Analyst:** These professionals gather and analyze threat intelligence from various sources to identify emerging threats, understand attacker motivations, and inform proactive security measures.

This list is not exhaustive, and new specializations emerge as the cybersecurity landscape evolves. It's important to explore different paths, identify your areas of interest, and continuously develop your knowledge and skills to stay ahead of the curve.

**Choosing Your Path:**

There's no single "best" path in cybersecurity. The ideal specialization for you depends on your interests, skills, and career goals. Here are some tips for choosing your path:

- **Consider your strengths and weaknesses:** What are you naturally good at? Do you enjoy hands-on work like penetration testing, or do you prefer a more analytical role like security analyst?

- **Research different specializations:** Learn about the responsibilities, skills, and career outlook for different cybersecurity paths.

- **Talk to professionals:** Connect with cybersecurity professionals on online forums or attend industry events to gain insights into various career paths.

- **Start with a broad foundation:** While specialization is valuable, a strong foundational knowledge of cybersecurity principles is essential for any path. Earning an entry-level certification and gaining general security experience can be a good starting point.

- **Stay curious and keep learning:** The cybersecurity landscape is constantly evolving. Commit to continuous learning to stay updated on the latest threats, vulnerabilities, and security best practices.

The world of cybersecurity offers a diverse and exciting range of career paths. By exploring different specializations, identifying your interests, and continuously honing your skills, you can carve your niche within this dynamic field and contribute to a more secure digital future.

This chapter has equipped you with a roadmap to navigate the various cybersecurity paths available. The next chapter will provide valuable resources to help you land your first cybersecurity role and kickstart your rewarding career in this ever-growing field.

# CHAPTER 6

## Developing Your Technical Skillset

This chapter will introduce you to some fundamental technical areas that many cybersecurity professionals leverage throughout their careers.

## 6.1 Operating System Security Hardening

Operating systems are the core software that manages computer hardware and resources. Security hardening refers to the process of configuring an operating system to make it more resistant to cyberattacks.

Here are some key aspects of operating system security hardening:

- **Disabling Unnecessary Services and Applications:** Minimizing the attack surface by disabling unnecessary services and applications that attackers might exploit.

- **Strong User Account Management:** Implementing strong password policies, enforcing least privilege principles (users only having the permissions they absolutely need), and disabling unused accounts.

- **Regular Security Patching:** Keeping operating systems and applications patched with the latest security updates is crucial to address known vulnerabilities.

- **Firewall Configuration:** Firewalls act as security barriers, filtering incoming and outgoing traffic based on predefined rules. Security hardening involves configuring firewalls to allow only authorized traffic.

- **Audit Logging and Monitoring:** Enabling audit logging allows you to track system activity and identify potential security incidents.

By following security hardening best practices for different operating systems (Windows, macOS, Linux), you gain a valuable skill that contributes to the overall security posture of any organization.

## 6.2 Linux Administration Fundamentals

Linux is a powerful and open-source operating system widely used in servers, network devices, and embedded systems. Having a foundational understanding of Linux administration is advantageous for many cybersecurity roles.

Here are some key areas of focus in Linux administration fundamentals:

- **Command Line Interface (CLI):** Unlike graphical user interfaces (GUIs) most users are accustomed to, Linux heavily relies on the command line for administration tasks. Mastering the CLI empowers you to navigate the system, manage files and permissions, and perform various administrative tasks efficiently.

- **User and Group Management:** Effectively managing users and groups on a Linux system is crucial for access control and security. This involves creating user accounts, assigning appropriate permissions, and adhering to security best practices.

- **Package Management:** Linux distributions use package managers to install, update, and remove software. Understanding package management tools like APT (Debian/Ubuntu) or Yum (Red Hat/CentOS) is essential for system administration.

- **File Permissions:** Understanding and managing file permissions on a Linux system determines who can access, modify, or delete files. Setting appropriate permissions is vital for data security.

- **Basic Shell Scripting:** Shell scripting allows you to automate repetitive tasks on a Linux system. Learning basic scripting languages like Bash can significantly improve your efficiency and streamline administrative workflows.

While a deep understanding of Linux administration might not be required for every cybersecurity role, possessing these fundamentals provides a strong foundation and opens doors to various opportunities within the field.

**6.3 Scripting for Automation (e.g., Python Scripting)**

Scripting languages empower you to automate repetitive tasks on a computer system. This skill is highly valuable in cybersecurity, where efficiency and automation are crucial aspects of many security processes.

- **Python Scripting:** Python is a popular, versatile scripting language widely used in cybersecurity due to its readability, extensive libraries, and large community support. Learning Python scripting equips you to automate tasks like data analysis, security information and event management (SIEM) log processing, and vulnerability scanning.
- **Other Scripting Languages:** While Python is a great starting point, other scripting languages like

Bash (for Linux shell scripting), PowerShell (widely used in Windows environments), and Ruby are also used for various automation purposes in cybersecurity.

By honing your scripting skills, you can significantly increase your efficiency and become a more valuable asset in any security team.

## 6.4 Cryptography and Encryption Techniques

Cryptography is the science of securing information through encryption and decryption techniques. Understanding these concepts is essential for safeguarding sensitive data in the digital world.

- **Encryption:** The process of transforming plain text data into an unreadable format using a cryptographic algorithm and a secret key. Only authorized individuals with the corresponding decryption key can access the original data.

- **Decryption:** The process of reversing the encryption process, transforming ciphertext back into its original plain text form using the decryption key.

- **Symmetric vs. Asymmetric Encryption:** Symmetric encryption uses a single secret key for both encryption and decryption. Asymmetric encryption uses a public/private key pair, where the public key encrypts data and the private key decrypts it.

Encryption plays a vital role in protecting data at rest (stored on devices) and in transit (transmitted over networks). Understanding different encryption algorithms and their applications is essential for many cybersecurity roles.

**Additional Technical Skills to Consider:**

Beyond the areas covered in this chapter, several other technical skills are valuable for cybersecurity professionals, depending on their chosen career path. Here are a few examples:

- **Network Security Fundamentals:** Understanding network protocols, TCP/IP stack concepts, firewalls, intrusion detection/prevention systems (IDS/IPS), and network segmentation is crucial for securing computer networks.

- **Web Application Security:** As web applications become increasingly prevalent, understanding web application vulnerabilities (e.g., SQL injection, Cross-Site Scripting – XSS) and secure coding practices is essential for protecting web-based systems.

- **Digital Forensics and Incident Response:** For those interested in investigating cybercrimes and responding to security incidents, skills in digital forensics evidence collection, analysis, and incident response procedures are invaluable.

- **Cloud Security:** With the rise of cloud computing, understanding cloud security best practices, cloud platform security features (e.g., AWS Security Groups, Azure Security Center), and compliance requirements is increasingly important.

- **Security Tools and Technologies:** Staying updated on the latest security tools and technologies used for vulnerability scanning, security information and event management (SIEM), penetration testing, and security orchestration, automation, and response (SOAR) is crucial for efficient security operations.

**Developing Your Skillset:**

The good news is that numerous resources are available to help you develop the technical skills needed for a successful cybersecurity career. Here are some tips to get you started:

- **Online Courses and Training Platforms:** Numerous reputable platforms offer online courses, tutorials, and certifications in various cybersecurity domains.

- **Books and Online Resources:** A wealth of books, articles, and online tutorials cover various technical topics in cybersecurity.

- **Hands-on Labs and Practice Environments:** Platforms offering simulated environments allow you to practice your skills in a safe, controlled setting. This is particularly valuable for learning penetration testing and security administration.

- **Open-Source Projects:** Contributing to open-source security projects can be a fantastic way to gain practical experience working with real-world security tools and technologies.

- **Home Labs:** Setting up a home lab allows you to experiment with different operating systems, security tools, and configurations in a controlled environment.

**Continuous Learning is Key:**

The cybersecurity landscape is constantly evolving. New threats emerge, and new technologies are developed. To stay relevant and competitive in this field, a commitment to continuous learning is essential.

Developing strong technical skillset is crucial for success in cybersecurity. By focusing on the core areas covered in this chapter and exploring additional specialties relevant to your chosen career path, you can equip yourself with the tools and knowledge required to excel in this dynamic field. Remember, the journey of learning never ends in cybersecurity. Embrace continuous learning, stay curious, and keep honing your skills to become a valuable asset in protecting our digital world.

# CHAPTER 7

## ADVANCED CERTIFICATIONS AND CONTINUED LEARNING

Now that you've grasped the fundamentals of cybersecurity, explored career paths, and begun developing your technical skillset, it's time to delve into advanced learning opportunities. This chapter will guide you on pursuing advanced certifications, staying abreast of industry trends, and building a strong cybersecurity learning community.

## 7.1 (ISC)² Certified Information Systems Security Professional (CISSP)

The (ISC)² CISSP is widely regarded as the gold standard

certification for experienced information security professionals. It validates your comprehensive knowledge and expertise across a broad range of security domains.

### 7.1.1 Earning the CISSP: Benefits and Challenges

**Benefits:**

- **Industry Recognition:** The CISSP is a globally recognized credential that demonstrates your expertise to potential employers and enhances your resume.

- **Career Advancement:** Earning the CISSP can open doors to senior security positions and command higher salaries.

- **Knowledge Validation:** The CISSP certification process validates your in-depth understanding of essential security principles and best practices.

- **Professional Development:** Preparing for the CISSP broadens your knowledge base and keeps you updated on the latest security trends.

## Challenges:

- **Experience Requirement:** The CISSP requires a minimum of five years of cumulative paid work experience in two or more of the eight domains covered by the CISSP Common Body of Knowledge (CBK).

- **Exam Difficulty:** The CISSP exam is notoriously challenging, requiring dedicated studying and preparation.

- **Cost:** The cost of the CISSP exam and associated training materials can be a significant investment.

## Tips for Success:

- **Meet the experience requirement:** Ensure you possess the required work experience before pursuing the CISSP.

- **Develop a study plan:** Create a comprehensive study plan that allocates time for each CISSP domain.

- **Utilize various resources:** Supplement your studies with official CISSP resources, practice tests, and online communities.

- **Join a CISSP bootcamp:** Consider enrolling in a bootcamp for intensive review and exam preparation guidance.

**Remember:** Earning the CISSP is a significant achievement that demonstrates your dedication to the cybersecurity field.

## 7.2 Certifications for Specific Security Domains

Beyond the CISSP, numerous advanced certifications cater to specific cybersecurity domains. Here are a few examples:

- **(ISC)$^2$ Certified Secure Incident Analyst (CSA+):** Ideal for individuals specializing in incident response, threat detection, and security operations.

- **GIAC Security Essentials (GSEC):** Provides a

broad foundation in information security and risk management, serving as a stepping stone towards more advanced GIAC certifications.

- **CompTIA Security+ Cloud Security Practitioner (CCSP):** Validates your expertise in securing cloud environments.

- **Certified Ethical Hacker (CEH):** Focuses on penetration testing methodologies and ethical hacking techniques.

These are just a few examples, and the best choice for you depends on your career goals and areas of specialization. Researching various advanced certifications aligned with your chosen path will help you select the ones that best compliment your skillset and career aspirations.

## 7.3 Staying Up-to-Date with Industry Trends and Threats

The cybersecurity landscape is constantly evolving. New threats emerge, vulnerabilities are discovered, and best practices change. To remain relevant and effective in your field, it's crucial to stay updated with industry trends and threats. Here are some ways to achieve this:

- **Follow Cybersecurity Blogs and News Websites:** Subscribe to reputable cybersecurity blogs and news websites to stay informed about the latest threats, vulnerabilities, and security incidents.

- **Attend Industry Conferences and Events:** Participating in conferences and events allows you to network with other professionals, learn about emerging technologies, and gain insights from industry leaders.

- **Take Advantage of Free Webinars and Trainings:** Many security vendors and organizations offer free webinars and training sessions on various security topics.

- **Join Online Security Communities:** Participating in online forums and communities allows you to connect with other cybersecurity professionals, share knowledge, and discuss industry trends.

By actively engaging with these resources, you can ensure your knowledge and skills remain current and relevant in the ever-evolving world of cybersecurity.

## 7.4 Building a Strong Cybersecurity Learning Community

A strong learning community can be a valuable asset in your cybersecurity journey. Here's how to build one:

- **Connect with Colleagues:** Network with colleagues in your organization and share knowledge and resources.

- **Join Online Forums and Groups:** Participate in online forums and groups dedicated to cybersecurity discussions and knowledge sharing.

- **Find a Cybersecurity Mentor:** Seek guidance and mentorship from experienced cybersecurity professionals.

- **Attend Local Meetups and Events:** Attend local meetups and events to connect with other security professionals in your area.

Surrounding yourself with a supportive and knowledgeable community can significantly enhance your learning experience and career growth in cybersecurity. Here are some additional benefits of building a strong learning community:

- **Motivation and Support:** Sharing your learning journey with others can provide motivation, especially during challenging times.

- **Knowledge Sharing and Collaboration:** Engaging with other professionals allows you to learn from their experiences, share your own knowledge, and collaborate on projects.

- **Exposure to Diverse Perspectives:** A diverse learning community exposes you to different viewpoints and approaches to security challenges, broadening your understanding of the field.

- **Career Opportunities:** Networking with other professionals can lead to new job opportunities and career advancements.

## How to Find Your Cybersecurity Community:

There are numerous avenues to build your cybersecurity learning community. Here are a few suggestions:

- **Online Forums and Communities:** Platforms like Reddit (r/cybersecurity), Discord servers dedicated to cybersecurity, and online communities hosted by security vendors offer vibrant discussions and knowledge sharing.
- **Social Media:** Follow cybersecurity professionals and organizations on LinkedIn and Twitter to stay updated on industry trends and connect with others.
- **Local Cybersecurity Meetups and Events:** Many cities host regular cybersecurity meetups and conferences. Attending these events allows you to connect with local professionals face-to-face.

- **Professional Organizations:** Joining professional organizations like (ISC)² or ISACA provides access to resources, events, and networking opportunities.

**Remember:** Building a strong learning community takes time and effort. Be proactive in engaging with others, participate in discussions, and contribute your own knowledge to create a mutually beneficial learning environment.

## 7.5 Lifelong Learning in Cybersecurity

The cybersecurity field is dynamic and ever-evolving. As new threats emerge, technologies advance, and best practices change, continuous learning is essential for a successful and fulfilling career in this domain.

# CHAPTER 8

## PRACTICAL EXPERIENCE AND PORTFOLIO BUILDING

This chapter will explore various methods to gain hands-on experience and demonstrate your capabilities in the cybersecurity field.

## 8.1 Home Labs and Virtualization

Home labs are simulated environments you create on your personal computer to practice and experiment with security tools, configurations, and security concepts in a safe and controlled setting.

**Benefits of Home Labs:**

- **Hands-on Learning:** Home labs provide a valuable platform to apply theoretical knowledge and gain practical experience with various security tools and technologies.

- **Testing and Experimentation:** You can freely test security tools, configurations, and procedures without risk of impacting production systems.

- **Building Confidence:** Successfully setting up and managing a home lab boosts your confidence and demonstrates your ability to apply your technical skills in a practical setting.

**Virtualization Tools:**

Virtualization software allows you to create multiple virtual machines on a single physical machine, enabling you to simulate complex network environments within your home lab. Popular virtualization tools include:

- **VMware Workstation Player (Free):** A free and widely used virtualization platform for personal use.

- **VirtualBox (Free):** Another popular open-source virtualization platform with a large user community.

- **Microsoft Hyper-V (Free with Windows Pro and Enterprise editions):** A built-in virtualization solution for Windows users.

**Home Lab Ideas:**

- **Deploy a Security Information and Event Management (SIEM) system:** Set up a SIEM system like ELK Stack (Elasticsearch, Logstash, Kibana) to collect and analyze logs from various simulated systems.

- **Build a Secure Network Environment:** Configure firewalls, intrusion detection systems (IDS), and network segmentation within your virtual network to practice security principles.

- **Practice Penetration Testing Techniques:** Utilize tools like Kali Linux to learn about vulnerability scanning, penetration testing methodologies, and ethical hacking techniques in a controlled environment.

Remember, your home lab doesn't require expensive hardware. Start with what you have and gradually expand your environment as your skills and resources grow.

## 8.2 Capture the Flag (CTF) Competitions

Capture the Flag (CTF) competitions are gamified cybersecurity events where participants compete to solve security challenges that involve tasks like cryptography, vulnerability analysis, web application security, and reverse engineering.

**Benefits of CTFs:**

- **Apply Skills in a Competitive Setting:** CTFs provide an engaging platform to test your skills against other security enthusiasts, identify areas for improvement, and learn from the approaches of others.

- **Teamwork and Collaboration:** Many CTFs encourage participation in teams, fostering collaboration and communication skills valuable in the professional cybersecurity world.

- **Building a Portfolio:** Strong performance in CTFs demonstrates your problem-solving skills, technical aptitude, and ability to think creatively under pressure.

## Finding CTFs:

Numerous CTF platforms and websites host competitions for all skill levels. Here are a few resources to get you started:

- **CTFtime:** A website that aggregates information about upcoming CTF competitions worldwide.

- **HackerRank:** Offers CTF challenges for various

difficulty levels.

- **Sans Institute:** Conducts CTF competitions throughout the year.

**Tips for Success in CTFs:**

- **Start with Beginner-Friendly CTFs:** As you gain experience, gradually progress to more challenging competitions.

- **Team Up with Others:** Participating in a team with complementary skillsets can significantly enhance your chances of success.

- **Practice Regularly:** The more you participate in CTFs, the more comfortable and confident you'll become in solving security challenges.

- **Learn from Your Mistakes:** Analyze your performance after each CTF to identify areas for improvement and enhance your skills for future competitions.

## 8.3 Security Bug Bounty Programs

Many organizations offer bug bounty programs, incentivizing security researchers to discover and report vulnerabilities in their systems and applications.

**Benefits of Bug Bounties:**

- **Gain Real-World Experience:** Participating in bug bounty programs allows you to identify and report real-world vulnerabilities, mimicking the work of professional security researchers.

- **Earn Rewards:** Some bug bounty programs offer financial rewards for discovering and reporting critical vulnerabilities. This can be a great way to supplement your income or gain recognition for your skills.

- **Build Your Reputation:** Successfully finding and reporting vulnerabilities can enhance your reputation within the security community and attract attention from potential employers.

**Finding Bug Bounty Programs:**

Several platforms list active bug bounty programs from various organizations. Here are a few examples:

- **HackerOne:** A leading bug bounty platform connecting organizations with security researchers.
- **Bugcrowd:** Another popular platform facilitating bug bounty programs for organizations of all sizes.
- **GitHub Security Lab:** Identifies and discloses security vulnerabilities in popular open-source projects hosted on GitHub.

**Responsible Disclosure:**

When participating in bug bounty programs, it's crucial to adhere to responsible disclosure practices. This involves:

- **Reporting vulnerabilities directly to the organization through designated channels.**
- **Providing sufficient information for the organization to replicate and address the vulnerability.**
- **Avoiding public disclosure of the vulnerability**

**until the organization has had a reasonable time to fix it.**

**Remember:** Always follow the program guidelines and terms of service set by each organization before participating in their bug bounty program.

## 8.4 Open Source Security Project Contributions

Contributing to open-source security projects is a fantastic way to gain practical experience, demonstrate your skills, and build a strong portfolio.

**Benefits of Open Source Security Projects:**

- **Learn from Experienced Developers:** Contributing to established open-source security projects allows you to collaborate with experienced developers and learn from their expertise.

- **Enhance Your Coding Skills:** The active development environment of open-source projects provides opportunities to improve your coding skills by working on real-world security tools and applications.

- **Build a Public Portfolio:** Your contributions to open-source projects become part of a public repository, showcasing your coding abilities and commitment to the security community.

**Finding Open Source Security Projects:**

Numerous open-source security projects exist on platforms like GitHub. Here's how to find suitable projects to contribute to:

- **Search for projects related to your areas of interest:** Focus on projects aligned with your technical skills and career goals.

- **Start by contributing small bug fixes or improvements:** Look for beginner-friendly tasks within larger projects to ease yourself into the contribution process.

- **Engage with the project community:** Actively

participate in project discussions, seek guidance from mentors, and demonstrate your dedication to contributing.

**Tips for Successful Open Source Contributions:**

- **Understand the project's codebase:** Familiarize yourself with the project's code structure, coding conventions, and contribution guidelines before diving in.

- **Communicate effectively:** Clearly document your code changes, provide detailed explanations in pull requests, and actively participate in project discussions.

- **Be patient and persistent:** Contributing to open-source projects can be an iterative process. Be patient, learn from feedback, and keep refining your contributions.

Building practical experience and a compelling portfolio is crucial for success in the cybersecurity field. By leveraging home labs, participating in CTFs, exploring bug bounty programs, and contributing to open-source security projects, you can demonstrate your skills, gain valuable experience, and stand out from the competition. Remember, the journey of learning and building your portfolio is ongoing. Embrace continuous learning, actively seek opportunities to showcase your skills, and don't be afraid to step outside your comfort zone.

CHAPTER 9

JOB SEARCH STRATEGIES AND INTERVIEW PREPARATION

This chapter will guide you through crafting a compelling resume and cover letter, mastering the art of cybersecurity job interviews, building valuable industry connections, and negotiating your worth in the job market.

## 9.1 Crafting a Compelling Cybersecurity Resume

Your resume is often the first impression you make on a potential employer. Here's how to create a cybersecurity resume that effectively showcases your skills and experience:

- **Tailor Your Resume for Each Job:** Carefully analyze the job description and highlight skills and experience directly relevant to the specific role.

- **Use Strong Action Verbs:** Replace generic verbs with action verbs that emphasize your accomplishments. For example, instead of "configured firewalls," use "implemented and maintained firewall configurations for a network of 500+ devices."

- **Quantify Your Achievements Whenever Possible:** Use numbers and metrics to quantify your accomplishments and demonstrate the impact of your work. For example, "Reduced security incidents by 20% through implementing a new intrusion detection system."

- **Highlight Relevant Certifications and Skills:** List certifications relevant to the position and showcase your technical skills using keywords from the job description.

- **Focus on Achievements, not Just Responsibilities:** Don't just list your job duties. Focus on what you achieved in each role and the positive impact you made.

- **Proofread Carefully:** Typos and grammatical errors can create a negative impression. Ensure your resume is error-free and professionally formatted.

**Additional Tips:**

- **Consider Including a Cybersecurity Skills Section:** List key technical skills relevant to the field, such as network security, vulnerability scanning, or incident response.

- **Tailor Your Resume Format for Applicant Tracking Systems (ATS):** Many companies use ATS to filter resumes. Use relevant keywords throughout your resume to ensure it passes through ATS scans.

- **Keep Your Resume Concise and Easy to Read:** Aim for a one- to two-page resume, depending on your experience level. Use clear headings, bullet points, and white space for readability.

By following these tips, you can create a compelling cybersecurity resume that grabs the attention of hiring managers and increases your chances of landing an interview.

## 9.2 Mastering the Art of Cybersecurity Job Interviews

Job interviews present an opportunity to showcase your expertise, enthusiasm, and cultural fit for the role. Here's how to prepare for and excel in your cybersecurity job interviews:

- **Research the Company and Position:** Thoroughly research the company's mission, values, and security practices. Understand the specific role you're interviewing for and its responsibilities.

- **Practice Common Cybersecurity Interview Questions:** Prepare for common cybersecurity interview questions such as explaining security concepts, describing your experience with specific tools, or outlining your approach to handling security incidents. Tools like mock interview platforms or practicing with a friend can be very helpful.

- **Prepare Your Own Questions:** Develop thoughtful questions for the interviewer demonstrating your genuine interest in the role and the company.

- **Dress Professionally:** First impressions matter. Dress professionally and appropriately for the company culture.

- **Be Confident and Enthusiastic:** Project confidence and enthusiasm for cybersecurity. Show your passion for the field and your desire to learn and contribute.

**Additional Tips:**

- **Highlight Your Soft Skills:** Cybersecurity isn't just about technical skills. Emphasize soft skills such as communication, teamwork, problem-solving, and critical thinking.

- **Be Prepared to Discuss Your Portfolio:** If you've built a portfolio through home labs, CTFs, or open-source contributions, be prepared to discuss these projects and the skills they demonstrate.

- **Follow Up After the Interview:** Send a thank-you email to the interviewer within 24 hours, reiterating your interest in the position and highlighting key points from the discussion.

By following these strategies, you can approach your cybersecurity job interviews with confidence and significantly increase your chances of landing your dream job.

## 9.3 Networking and Building Industry Connections

Building strong industry connections can be a valuable asset in your job search. Here's how to network effectively within the cybersecurity field:

- **Attend Industry Events and Conferences:** Participating in conferences, meetups, and workshops allows you to connect with other cybersecurity professionals, learn from industry leaders, and potentially meet potential employers.

- **Join Online Communities and Forums:** Engage in online cybersecurity forums and communities. This allows you to share knowledge, connect with others, and stay updated on industry trends.

- **Connect with Professionals on LinkedIn (continued):** Build your network on LinkedIn by connecting with cybersecurity professionals, following companies you're interested in, and joining relevant LinkedIn groups.

- **Inform Your Network of Your Job Search:** Let your network know you're actively seeking a cybersecurity role. They may be aware of open positions or connect you with relevant people in their network.

- **Consider Mentorship Programs:** Mentorship programs can connect you with experienced cybersecurity professionals who can offer guidance, support, and career advice.

**Remember:** Networking is a two-way street. Offer value to your network by sharing your knowledge, providing helpful insights, and being a supportive connection for others.

## 9.4 Salary Negotiation Tips for Cybersecurity Professionals

Cybersecurity professionals are in high demand, and salaries can be quite competitive. Here are some tips for negotiating your salary in a cybersecurity job offer:

- **Research Market Rates:** Before entering

negotiation, research average salaries for similar cybersecurity positions in your geographic location and with your experience level. Salary comparison websites and industry reports can be helpful resources.

- **Understand Your Worth:** Consider your skills, experience, certifications, and the value you bring to the role.

- **Be Confident and Professional:** Approach the negotiation with confidence and professionalism. Clearly articulate your value proposition and why you deserve the salary you're requesting.

- **Be Prepared to Walk Away:** Know your bottom line and be prepared to walk away from the offer if it doesn't meet your expectations.

**Additional Tips:**

- **Negotiate More Than Just Salary:** Consider negotiating benefits such as health insurance, vacation time, professional development opportunities, or signing bonuses in addition to base salary.

- **Get Everything in Writing:** Once you've reached an agreement, ensure all details, including salary, benefits, and start date, are clearly outlined in a written employment contract.

By following these tips, you can confidently negotiate your salary in a cybersecurity job offer and ensure you're compensated fairly for your skills and expertise.

Landing your dream job in cybersecurity requires dedication, preparation, and a strategic approach. This chapter has equipped you with valuable strategies for crafting a compelling resume and cover letter, mastering job interviews, building strong industry connections, and negotiating your worth in the job market. Remember, job hunting is a journey, not a destination. Stay focused, leverage the resources available to you, and don't give up on your pursuit of a successful cybersecurity career. With hard work, perseverance, and the knowledge you've gained throughout this guide, you'll be well on your way to achieving your goals in this exciting and ever-evolving field.

## CHAPTER 10

### THE FUTURE OF CYBERSECURITY

You've gained a comprehensive understanding of cybersecurity fundamentals, explored career paths, honed your technical skills, and learned valuable strategies for launching your career in this dynamic field. As you embark on your cybersecurity journey, it's crucial to stay informed about the ever-evolving landscape of threats and technologies. This chapter will explore emerging security challenges associated with new technologies, the evolving role of cybersecurity professionals, and the importance of continuous learning in this ever-changing domain.

## 10.1 Emerging Technologies and Security Challenges

The rapid advancement of technology presents both exciting opportunities and significant security challenges. Here, we'll delve into three key areas with growing security concerns:

### 10.1.1 Cloud Security

Cloud computing has revolutionized the way businesses store data and access applications. However, this shift introduces new security considerations:

- **Shared Responsibility Model:** In cloud environments, the security responsibility is shared between the cloud provider and the organization using the cloud service. It's critical to understand this model and implement appropriate security measures on your end.

- **Data Security in the Cloud:** Ensuring the confidentiality, integrity, and availability of data stored in the cloud requires robust security controls and encryption strategies.

- **Misconfiguration Risks:** Improper configuration of cloud resources can create vulnerabilities and expose sensitive data.

**Security Best Practices for Cloud Environments:**

- **Implement strong access controls and identity management.**

- **Encrypt sensitive data at rest and in transit.**

- **Regularly monitor and audit cloud activity for suspicious behavior.**

- **Stay updated on cloud security best practices and adhere to compliance requirements.**

## 10.1.2 Internet of Things (IoT) Security

The Internet of Things (IoT) refers to the vast network of interconnected devices collecting and sharing data. While IoT offers numerous benefits, it also presents unique security challenges:

- **Resource-Constrained Devices:** Many IoT devices have limited processing power and memory, making it difficult to implement traditional security solutions.

- **Insecure Communication Protocols:** Some IoT devices rely on insecure communication protocols, allowing attackers to intercept data or take control of devices.

- **Large Attack Surface:** The sheer number and variety of IoT devices create a vast attack surface for malicious actors to exploit.

**Securing the IoT Ecosystem:**

- **Choose devices with robust security features and**

**encryption capabilities.**

- **Keep device software updated with the latest security patches.**

- **Segment IoT devices on a separate network from critical systems.**

- **Implement strong authentication and authorization mechanisms for IoT devices.**

## 10.1.3 Artificial Intelligence (AI) Security

Artificial intelligence (AI) is rapidly transforming various industries. However, AI systems can also be vulnerable to security threats:

- **AI Bias and Discrimination:** AI algorithms can perpetuate biases present in the data they are trained on, leading to discriminatory outcomes.

- **Adversarial Attacks:** Malicious actors can manipulate AI systems with specially crafted inputs, causing them to produce inaccurate or harmful outputs.

- **Security of AI Infrastructure:** The security of the underlying infrastructure supporting AI systems, such as cloud platforms and data pipelines, is crucial to ensure overall system integrity.

**Securing AI Systems:**

- **Use diverse and unbiased datasets to train AI models.**
- **Implement robust security measures to protect AI systems from adversarial attacks.**
- **Regularly audit and monitor AI systems for potential biases and security vulnerabilities.**

These are just a few examples of how emerging technologies are shaping the cybersecurity landscape. As technology continues to evolve, so too will the threats and challenges we face.

## 10.2 The Evolving Role of Cybersecurity Professionals

The role of cybersecurity professionals is constantly

adapting to meet the demands of the ever-changing threat landscape. Here's what you can expect:

- **Focus on Specializations:** As security concerns become more specialized, professionals with deep expertise in specific areas like cloud security, IoT security, or AI security will be increasingly sought after.

- **Automation and Orchestration:** Security professionals will leverage automation and security orchestration and automation (SOAR) tools to streamline tasks and focus on strategic initiatives.

- **Collaboration with Other Departments:** Effective cybersecurity requires collaboration across departments. Security professionals will need strong communication and problem-solving skills to work effectively with IT, engineering, and other teams.

**Staying Relevant in the Evolving Landscape:**

- **Continuously update your skills and knowledge:**

Pursue advanced certifications, attend industry conferences, and stay updated on the latest threats and technologies.

- **Embrace a growth mindset:** Be adaptable and willing to learn new skills as the cybersecurity landscape evolves.

- **Develop strong communication and collaboration skills:** Effectively communicate security risks to non-technical audiences and collaborate with other teams to implement security solutions.

## 10.3 Continuous Learning and Staying Ahead of the Curve

The cybersecurity field is dynamic and ever-evolving. New threats emerge, technologies advance, and best practices change at a rapid pace. To remain relevant and thrive in this dynamic environment, continuous learning is essential for any cybersecurity professional. Here are some strategies to stay ahead of the curve:

- **Pursue Advanced Certifications:** Certifications validate your expertise in specific security domains and demonstrate your commitment to professional development. Consider pursuing advanced certifications aligned with your career goals and the evolving security landscape.

- **Attend Industry Conferences and Events:** Participating in conferences, workshops, and meetups allows you to network with other professionals, learn about emerging threats and technologies from industry leaders, and discover new trends and best practices.

- **Take Advantage of Online Resources:** Numerous online resources such as security blogs, webinars, and training platforms offer valuable learning opportunities. Subscribe to reputable sources, participate in online courses, and leverage free training materials to stay updated on the latest developments.

- **Engage with Online Communities:** Join online

forums, communities, and discussion groups dedicated to cybersecurity. Interacting with other professionals allows you to share knowledge, learn from their experiences, and keep pace with industry trends.

- **Contribute to Open-Source Security Projects:** Contributing to open-source security projects provides hands-on experience with real-world security challenges, allows you to collaborate with experienced developers, and positions you as a thought leader within the community.

**Embrace a Growth Mindset:**

A critical aspect of continuous learning is adopting a growth mindset. This means believing that your skills and knowledge can be developed through effort and dedication. By approaching challenges with a willingness to learn and adapt, you'll be well-positioned to navigate the ever-changing cybersecurity landscape.

## 10.4 Building a Rewarding and Fulfilling Cybersecurity Career

A career in cybersecurity can be both intellectually stimulating and personally rewarding. Here's why you might find cybersecurity fulfilling:

- **Constant Learning and Challenge:** The field of cybersecurity offers continuous learning opportunities and intellectual challenges that keep your work engaging and stimulating.

- **Making a Positive Impact:** By protecting businesses and individuals from cyber threats, you play a vital role in safeguarding critical infrastructure and data.

- **High Demand and Job Security:** Cybersecurity professionals are in high demand, and the job market outlook is strong. This translates to greater job security and potential for career advancement.

- **Diverse Career Paths:** The cybersecurity field offers a wide range of career paths, allowing you to specialize in areas that align with your interests and skillset.

- **Sense of Accomplishment:** Successfully mitigating security threats and protecting sensitive information can provide a strong sense of accomplishment and personal satisfaction.

**Remember:** While cybersecurity can be challenging, it is also a rewarding and fulfilling field for those who are passionate about technology and security. By embracing continuous learning, staying updated on the latest trends, and actively contributing to the community, you can build a successful and impactful career in this exciting domain.

This comprehensive guide has equipped you with the knowledge, resources, and strategies to launch a successful career in cybersecurity. As you embark on your journey, remember that cybersecurity is a lifelong learning endeavor. Embrace the challenge, stay curious, and keep exploring the vast and ever-rewarding world of cybersecurity. There's no doubt that with dedication, perseverance, and the skills you've gained throughout this guide, you'll achieve your goals and make a significant contribution to this critical field.

**Congratulations!** You've completed this comprehensive guide to launching your cybersecurity career. We wish you the very best in your exciting journey ahead!

# ABOUT THE AUTHOR

Writer's Bio:

 Benjamin Evans, a respected figure in the tech world, is known for his insightful commentary and analysis. With a strong educational background likely in fields such as computer science, engineering, or business, he brings a depth of knowledge to his discussions on emerging technologies and industry trends. Evans' knack for simplifying complex concepts, coupled with his innate curiosity and passion for innovation, has established him as a go-to source for understanding the dynamics of the digital landscape. Through articles, speeches, and social media, he shares his expertise and offers valuable insights into the impact of technology on society.

www.ingramcontent.com/pod-product-compliance
Lightning Source LLC
LaVergne TN
LVHW022125060326
832903LV00063B/4026